THE CINCINNATI BENGALS

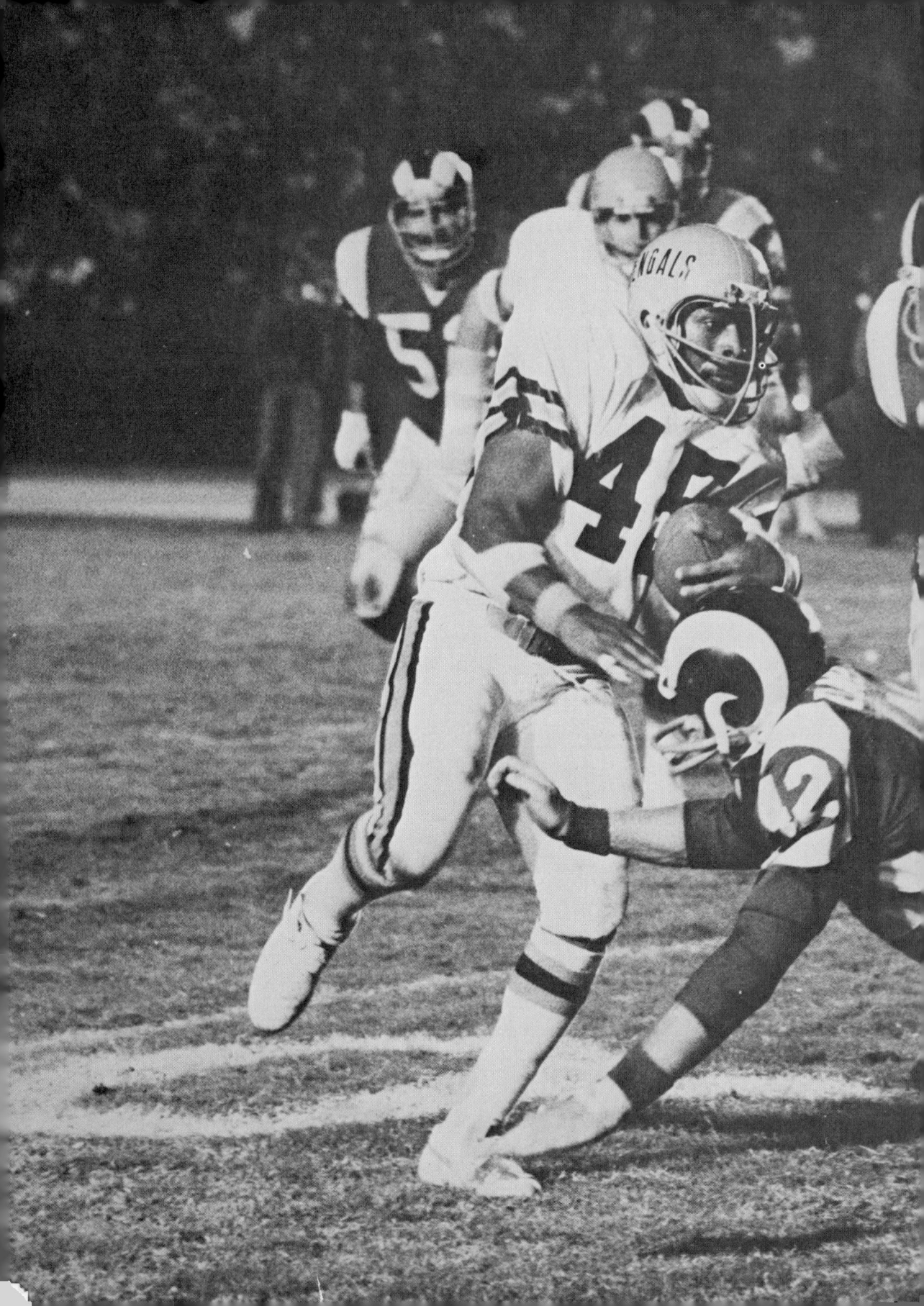

Published by Creative Education, Inc., 123 South Broad Street, Mankato, Minnesota 56001

Copyright © 1986 by Creative Education, Inc. International copyrights reserved in all countries. No part of this book may be reproduced in any form without written permission from the publisher. Printed in the United States.

Library of Congress Catalog Card No.: 85-72610

ISBN: 0-88682-028-6

85 629

7623

THE CINCINNATI BENGALS

JAMES R. ROTHAUS

CREATIVE EDUCATION

Coach Paul Brown always kept a tight rein on his players.

NEW START FOR AN OLD LEGEND

The pages of football history are checkered with the names of strong-willed men who seemed to possess the God-given gift of leadership. We call these men "coaches," but we could just as easily call them father, brother, friend and inspiration—for they were usually all this and more to the young athletes who played for them.

Over the years, there has been a handful of outstanding coaches who have become legends in their own communities, but there is one among them whose reputation roared across the entire nation and still lingers in the hearts and minds of football fans from coast-to-coast. That man is Paul Brown, and he is still honored as one of the all-time winningest coaches in football history, having racked up 361 victories over the incredible span of 41 seasons of high school, collegiate and professional football.

Paul Brown is the only man ever to have a National Football League team—the Cleveland Browns—named after him. Brown built that franchise from the ground up. But, as we shall soon see, he was also responsible for building another great Ohio franchise—the Cincinnati Bengals—into a perennial power.

The Paul Brown legend began to unfold way back in 1930 when he first pulled on an old gray sweatshirt and began coaching high school football in Ohio. Even then,

Did you know?

When Paul Brown was inducted into the Pro Football Hall-of-Fame in 1967, he was cited not only for his unequalled coaching record but as "the first to make coaching a fulltime profession, not only for himself, but for a staff of assistants, a practice that has now become universal."

> **Did you know?**
>
> *"Benzoo" is a majestic Bengal Tiger that resides at the Cincinnati Zoo on Monday thru Saturday. On Sundays, of course, Benzoo can be seen at Riverfront Stadium in his official role as Bengals mascot!*

he seemed to have a special knack for molding average athletes into superbly-polished stars. Over the next decade Brown moved up and on into the college ranks and—sure enough—he directed Ohio State University to the collegiate national championship.

On and on, higher and higher, Brown's teams continued to claim the top prize. As the Cleveland Browns' mentor in the old All American Football Conference, he guided the team to four consecutive titles. Then, in 1950, when the AAFC merged with the NFL, Brown's upstart team defeated the mighty Philadelphia Eagles for the league title. Actually, it was the first of three league championships and six divisional titles that Cleveland would claim with Brown at the helm.

But this is the story of the exciting events that occurred after Brown left Cleveland, supposedly "retiring" from coaching forever. It's the story of Paul Brown's comeback, of how he founded a new NFL expansion team called the Cincinnati Bengals, and of how the brash young Bengals went on to carve out their own turf in the rough, tough world of the NFL giants.

HOW THE BENGALS GOT THEIR START

Down deep inside, Paul Brown had been itching to get back into pro football ever since his departure from Cleveland in 1962. So, in 1968 when Ohio Governor James Rhodes mentioned the possibility of a new team on the banks of the Ohio River, the old legend jumped at the opportunity.

For eleven seasons, center Bob Johnson was captain of the Cincinnati offense. He retired in 1978 after an outstanding career.

Players carry Coach Paul Brown off the field after the Bengals won the 1970 Central Division title.

Even before he signed his first player, Brown began working minor miracles. On his word alone, the Cincinnati City Council approved a big budget to build the brand-new 60,000-seat Riverfront Stadium. The Bengals hadn't even played their first game and already they boasted one of the finest stadiums in pro sports.

Things didn't go quite so smoothly out on the playing field, however. With Brown doing "triple duty" as the team's owner, general manager and head coach, the Bengals lost 11 of 14 games during that first season.

"Maybe Brown is spreading himself too thin," grumbled the Cincinnati fans. "Maybe he should've stuck to simply owning and running the club. Maybe he's lost the old coaching magic."

Not so. Looking back over the disappointing 1968 season, Brown saw promise where others saw only failure. He saw, for example, that several of those Bengal defeats had been near-victories right down to the final whistle. He saw that even though his team had been made up of raw rookies and aging NFL castoffs, those players had pulled together as a team, pushing through the hard times, holding their own against far better talent, and showing flashes of brilliance in the bargain.

Take rookie tailback Paul Robinson, for example. In only his seventh game as a pro, Robinson broke outside against Oakland and raced down the sidelines 87 yards for a touchdown. That run still ranks as the longest in Cincinnati history, and it was just one of the reasons Robinson rushed for over 1,000 yards to gain Rookie of the Year honors.

In 1969, guiding his rookies and NFL castoffs care-

Did you know?

On December 2, 1973, the Bengals blanked the mighty Minnesota Vikings, 27-0, in Riverfront Stadium. It was the first time in 162 games that the Vikings had been shut out!

11

Running back Paul Robinson grabs a piece of turf for the Bengals. He rolled up 1,023 yards during his rookie year.

Wounded Virgil Carter (left) and his backup, Ken Anderson, keep an eye on things from the sidelines.

Ka-pow! Tommy Casanova clobbers Mike Phipps of Cleveland.

fully from the sidelines, Paul Brown began to prove his stuff once again.

The Bengals roared off to a sizzling start, winning three in a row. In the third victory, they trounced the Kansas City Chiefs, who would go on to win Super Bowl IV. The Bengals only managed one more win that season, but that didn't prevent the people of Cincinnati from bragging about the exploits of Greg Cook.

Cook was a hometown favorite. He had played some pretty fair college ball at Cincinnati University, but then he had really blossomed with the Bengals. As a rookie, he led the AFL in passing. Old-timers still recall his four-touchdown performance in the win over Houston that season. He was the kind of young quarterback who could take a team to the championship on his coattails. Sadly, however, he never got a chance; his arm was severely injured by an awkward hit late in the season. After one brilliant year, Greg Cook's days as a QB were over.

JUST WHEN YOU LEAST EXPECT IT

Without Cook, the Bengals seemed destined to lose in 1970. Unsung Sam Wyche stepped up to starting quarterback, with a Chicago washout named Virgil Carter assuming the back-up role. To the surprise of all, this pair made a dynamite duo. Behind them, Cincinnati finished 8-6 and took the AFC Central Division title. All the people who had second-guessed Paul Brown

Did you know?

If you wonder what football players do with their spare time, consider Ross Browner's activities. He contributes time to Boys Club of Omaha, the NAACP, the United Negro College Fund, Big Brothers and Big Sisters, Bob Hope House, American Cancer Society, Boy Scouts, Independent Business Association, Notre Dame Alumni Club and Church of all Religions!

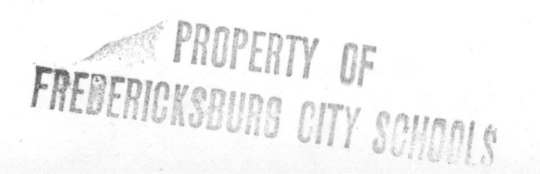

> **Did you know?**
>
> *Big, fast Bengals tackle, Anthony Munoz, landed a part in the hit movie, "The Right Stuff." Can you name the character he played? Hint: Munoz wore a white hospital uniform in the movie.*

were now red in the face. The Bengal coach was voted NFL Coach of the Year.

But that's just a sampling of the excitement that surrounded Cincinnati in 1970. The first big news came during training camp when over 40,000 fans bought season tickets. They sensed that something was brewing in Bengalville. They also wanted to see the city's impressive new stadium which had just opened.

Most of the time you couldn't find an empty seat at Bengal games. Sixty-thousand turned out to see Cincinnati trim cross-state rival Cleveland, and another full house was on hand when the Bengals wrapped up the division title with a rousing 45-7 win over the New England Patriots.

"Can you believe these fans?" said linebacker Bill Bergey, one of the league's outstanding young talents. "Even when we're just throwing the ball around before the game, they're on their feet yelling and screaming. It's just incredible."

Baltimore bumped off the Bengals in the first round of the playoffs, 17-0, but Brown predicted an even better year in 1971.

Things began well, as the Bengals easily defeated Philadelphia in the opener, but injuries besieged the team the rest of the year. First Carter was sidelined. Then it was the top draft choice, back-up quarterback Ken Anderson, who was felled. Finally the passing chores fell upon punter Dave Lewis, who had done a little quarterbacking in college. It's easy to see why the Bengals dropped to 4-10.

Boobie Clark slithers through the crush in a 1973 game against mighty Pittsburgh.

On November 3, 1974, the Colts met their doom, giving Coach Paul Brown of Cincinnati his 200th pro coaching victory. Here Ken Anderson's pass is deflected by Fred Cook, but recovered by Bengal stalwart Bob Johnson. Final score was Cincinnati 24, Baltimore 14.

THE PIANO-PLAYING PASS RUSHER

The Bengals rebounded in 1972 with another 8-6 record, which was good enough for second place in the AFC Central. Much of the improvement was attributed to the defense, particularly a piano-playing pass rusher named Mike Reid.

When the Bengals drafted Reid out of Penn State's football factory, they were looking for a mainstay at defensive tackle. They never expected to get a concert pianist out of the deal. Reid, a giant at 6-5, 260 pounds, could do both. In fact, he was a regular guest performer with the local symphony in Cincinnati.

Reid admitted it was a strange combination. "Sometimes I think I'll get my finger stepped on and that will be the end of my piano playing days," he said. "But I get paid more to play football, so I can't spend time worrying about it."

If anyone was worried, it was opposing quarterbacks. Reid was always chasing them out of the pocket. In 1972, he caught enough of them to be named All-Pro. Not bad for a concert musician.

Reid and the rest of the Bengals were poised for their best-ever season in 1973. Two splendid rookies—wide receiver Isaac Curtis and running back Charles (Boobie) Clark—added spark to the offense, which was bolstered by the rapid improvement of Ken Anderson. He and the entire Cincinnati team seemed to mature with each play.

In the second half of the season, the Bengals played defense with a vengeance. In a contest against the fabled

Did you know?

Louis Breeden led the Bengals in interceptions with seven during the 1980 season. The following year, Breeden intercepted a pass against San Diego and returned it 102 yards for a touchdown, thus tieing the NFL record for longest TD interception!

Lenvil Elliot rolls into the end zone for another Bengal score during the 1975 playoff against Oakland.

Paul Brown turned the head coaching job over to Bill "Tiger" Johnson (right) in 1976.

In one of many 1977 humiliations, Ken Anderson is hit by San Diego's Leroy Jones in the upset game of October 2, which Cincy lost, 24-3.

Minnesota Vikings, the Bengals could not be denied. Mike Reid and Sherman White put the elusive Fran Tarkenton under wraps. Cornerbacks Lamar Parrish and Tom Casanova shut down the Viking receivers. Meanwhile, Anderson and Curtis hooked up for one score and Clark rushed for two more as the Bengals crushed the Vikings, 27-0. It was the first time in over 11 years that Minnesota had been held scoreless!

The Central Division race went right down to the final day of the regular season. It wasn't until German-born placekicker Horst Muhlmann booted a fourth-quarter field goal to beat Houston that the Bengals finally prevailed, winning the title with a 10-4 record.

With that victory, the Bengals won the right to meet Super Bowl-bound Miami in the playoffs. The older, more experienced Dolphins drowned the Bengals, 34-16.

The next year, 1974, Cincinnati did well enough to finish 7-7, not a bad mark considering the team's two top rushers—Essex Johnson and Boobie Clark—were injured much of the time.

Both runners were back the following year. So was the red-hot passing combination of Anderson to speedy Isaac Curtis. Cincinnati broke out fast, winning its first six in a row. Had it not been for a late-season rush by Pittsburgh, the Bengals, 11-3, would have won another Central Division championship (The Steelers won it with a 12-2 mark).

Still, the Bengals secured a wild-card playoff berth and traveled to Oakland to meet the Raiders. It was a valiant effort by Cincinnati, but the Raiders were a litte too tough. They won, 31-28.

"Win or lose, I am very proud of this team," said Paul

Did you know?

The all-time Cincinnati scoring record is 115 points in a single season. It was set by the one-and-only Jim Breech in 1981, and he did it without scoring a single touchdown. Breech, of course, was the team's pressure-proof kicker!

> **Did you know?**
>
> *Isaac Curtis, the Bengals' fluid, graceful receiver, owns a beverage distributorship in Dayton, Ohio. His partner? Quarterback Ken Anderson!*

Brown. "They never give an inch, never quit." It made it all the more difficult for Brown to make his next statement.

SO NEAR, SO FAR

Four days later, Paul Brown announced that he would step down as head coach. He would continue as general manager of the club, but now the coaching reins would go to Bill "Tiger" Johnson, Brown's long-time assistant.

Johnson's first season almost ended in triumph. The Bengals clawed their way to a 10-4 record in 1976. Again, however, another late-season rush by the Steelers caught them at the wire, edging them out of the division title and the playoffs.

Cincinnati fell short of a post-season spot in 1977, as well. Nevertheless, the Bengals produced a number of league stars, including Tommy Casanova, the hard-hitting, go-for-broke safety, and Jim LeClair, the bone-crunching tackler who held down the middle linebacker position.

Halfway through the 1978 season, fans and players began to grumble. The Bengals has missed the playoffs in 1977 and were now on a five-game losing streak. Paul Brown had confidence in Coach Johnson, but not all the players did. Coy Bacon and Lamar Parrish, two Pro Bowl players, expressed their doubts out loud...and were promptly traded to Washington.

More woes: Bob Trumpy and Tom Casanova retired. Anderson broke his hand. Linebacker Bo Harris and running back Lenvil Elliott were also hurt.

Chris Bahr kicks another perfect field goal for the Bengals.

More bad luck: Kansas City won in the final minutes on a blocked punt. Cleveland came from behind to win in overtime. New Orleans squeaked by on a last-second field goal.

Reluctantly, Paul Brown decided to fire his good friend, Coach Johnson. Homer Rice, an assistant, was hired to replace him. Rice had his work cut out for him. He had been an outstanding college coach, but the NFL was a whole new ball game. Some people doubted that he was the right man to turn a losing team around. Others argued that Paul Brown was to blame. After all, Brown was still calling most of the shots.

> **Did you know?**
>
> *Off to a great start! Burly ball-carrier Larry Kinnebrew (6-1, 250 pounds) scored a touchdown against Cleveland the first time he carried the football in a National Football League game!*

PUTTING THE ROAR BACK IN THE BENGALS

Whatever the reason, Cincinnati immediately went into a tailspin in 1979. The Bengals literally couldn't beat anybody. Good teams and bad teams—they all defeated the Bengals. Rice was dumbfounded. He changed practice times. He switched defenses. He tried changing quarterbacks. He went with Anderson, then rookie Jack Thompson, then Anderson again. It seemed nothing worked. The only bright spots were provided by halfback Don Bass and battering-ram fullback Pete Johnson.

After the second consecutive 4-12 mark, Brown released Rice and his entire staff. This time, for a change, Brown didn't promote an assistant. Instead he went to the Canadian Football League and tapped Forrest Gregg.

Cincinnati cornerback Ken Riley grabs Minnesota wide receiver Ahmad Rashad (28) from behind after Rashad picked up ten second-quarter yards for the Vikings.

Rookie Don Bass scored a touchdown against New Orleans in a close 1978 contest—but the luckless Bengals snatched defeat from the jaws of victory and managed to lose, 20-18.

Bengal Lamar Parrish intercepts a pass to Steeler Lynn Swann in the exciting game of December 10, 1977.

Come to papa! Pat McInally scoops in the winning touchdown, giving Cincinnati a crucial win over the Steelers.

Here was a 15-year veteran of the NFL, a seasoned coach and a Hall-of-Famer. The legendary Vince Lombardi had described Gregg as "the finest player I ever coached."

The Bengals were quite a challenge for their new coach, but Forrest Gregg was equal to the task. By the start of regular-season play, the 1980 Bengals had all the earmarks of a winner. The schedule, though, was not an easy one, and it showed up in the early results. Tampa Bay tripped Cincinnati, 17-12; Miami won a close one, 17-16.

Game No. 3 brought on the Pittsburgh Steelers who were the defending Super Bowl champions. Anderson came out throwing—first a short one to tight end Dan Ross, then a long bomb to Isaac Curtis. Pete Johnson thundered up the middle. Late in the fourth quarter, it was the Bengals who held a slim, 30-28, lead. But Pittsburgh had the ball. On fourth down, with time running out, the Steelers had moved within field-goal range. The fans rose to their feet, and the Bengals defense bristled as the ball was snapped. Big Ross Browner bear-hugged the Steelers' Franco Harris and tossed him to the ground. No doubt about it, the bite was back in the Bengals!

Three weeks later, the Bengals traveled to Pittsburgh and defeated the champs again, this time in their own backyard. "When you beat the Steelers twice, you're accomplishing something," said a jubilant Forrest Gregg.

The Bengals' 6-10 record wasn't good enough for the playoffs, but it was a definite improvement, and they had beaten the World Champions twice.

Did you know?

Coy Bacon did it in 1976. He set a new club record by exploding for 26 quarterback sacks that year!

> **Did you know?**
>
> *Punter Pat McInnally writes a syndicated column— "Pat Answers For Kids" —for 80 different newspapers. He also enjoys songwriting, and is credited with writing the hit song, "Endlessly."*

BENGALS EARN THEIR STRIPES

There was a special feeling in the Bengals' camp in 1981. It was a good feeling, a winning feeling.

The Bengals knew they had the makings to go all the way. After all, they had already proven it by beating the Steelers twice the year before.

Paul Brown sensed this was a special team, so he decided to give them special uniforms. New pants, shirts, socks and helmets, all decorated with orange and black tiger stripes. "Now," said Coach Gregg, "it's time to go out and earn those stripes."

In the Bengals' first outing, however, the fierce Seattle Seahawks flew in their face. With Seattle on top, 21-0, at the half, Coach Gregg pulled Anderson and replaced him with back-up QB, Turk Schonert.

Young Schonert's go-get-em style injected new life into the offense. Believe it or not, the Bengals reeled off 27 straight points for the opening game victory. What a shot in the arm!

Anderson worked his way back into the starting role. He threw for three touchdowns to down Buffalo, 27-24, in overtime. Then he threw four TD strikes to give Cincinnati its fifth consecutive win, a satisfying 41-21 victory over the arch-rival Browns.

The Bengals were roaring. They hadn't been to the playoffs in six seasons. Just one more victory—against Pittsburgh—and the AFC Central Division would be theirs. The result? Bengals, 17; Steelers, 10!

Looking back on the '81 season, certain individual marks deserve special mention: Pete Johnson racked

Ross Browner (79), defender Scott Perry (right), and two other Bengals appear hopeful at last as the 1978 season starts looking up.

Smashed flat but still smiling, Tony Davis scores a touchdown for the Bengals.

up 1,077 yards and 16 touchdowns on the ground. Cris Collinsworth, Anderson's sure-handed favorite, caught eight TD passes. Anderson himself was tabbed the NFL's Player of the Year. Even the special teams kicked up a storm—punter Pat McInally and placekicker Jim Breech each set new club records!

A sellout crowd at Riverfront Stadium watched Cincinnati climb one step closer to the Super Bowl by defeating Buffalo.

Now, the Bengals would host San Diego in the AFC Championship Game at Riverfront. In the previous week, the Chargers had played in mild, 70-degree temperatures out West. This Sunday, the Bengals and the Chargers would duke it out in the worst possible conditions. There was wind-blown snow and the thermometer registered nine below zero. But it felt even colder. The wind-chill factor made it minus-59!

Anderson must have had anti-freeze in his arm that day. He drilled a series of perfect passes right into the hands of Collinsworth and Isaac Curtis. Pete Johnson's stump-like legs pumped through the San Diego line. On defense, Jim LeClair and Reggie Williams stopped Dan Fouts' Chargers cold. Despite the temperature, the 47,000 Bengal fans remained in their seats until the final scoreboard tally told the tale. Cincinnati's 27-7 win had launched the Bengals into the Super Bowl at last!

SUPER TIMES FOR CINCINNATI

For 14 long years, Cincinnati fans had waited for the day when their Bengals would finally make it to the

Did you know?

Wide receiver Steve Kreider is jokingly referred to as "The Professor" by his teammates, and no wonder. Kreider holds a Bachelor of Science degree and a Masters degree in business administration. He was Student of the Year and a Rhodes Scholar nominee at the University of California in 1983!

Archie Griffin took his lumps in the Falcon game, but he would star in a later 1978 contest against Cleveland.

In 1978, Bengal quarterback Ken Anderson had a completion percentage of 54.2 for total yardage of 2,219.

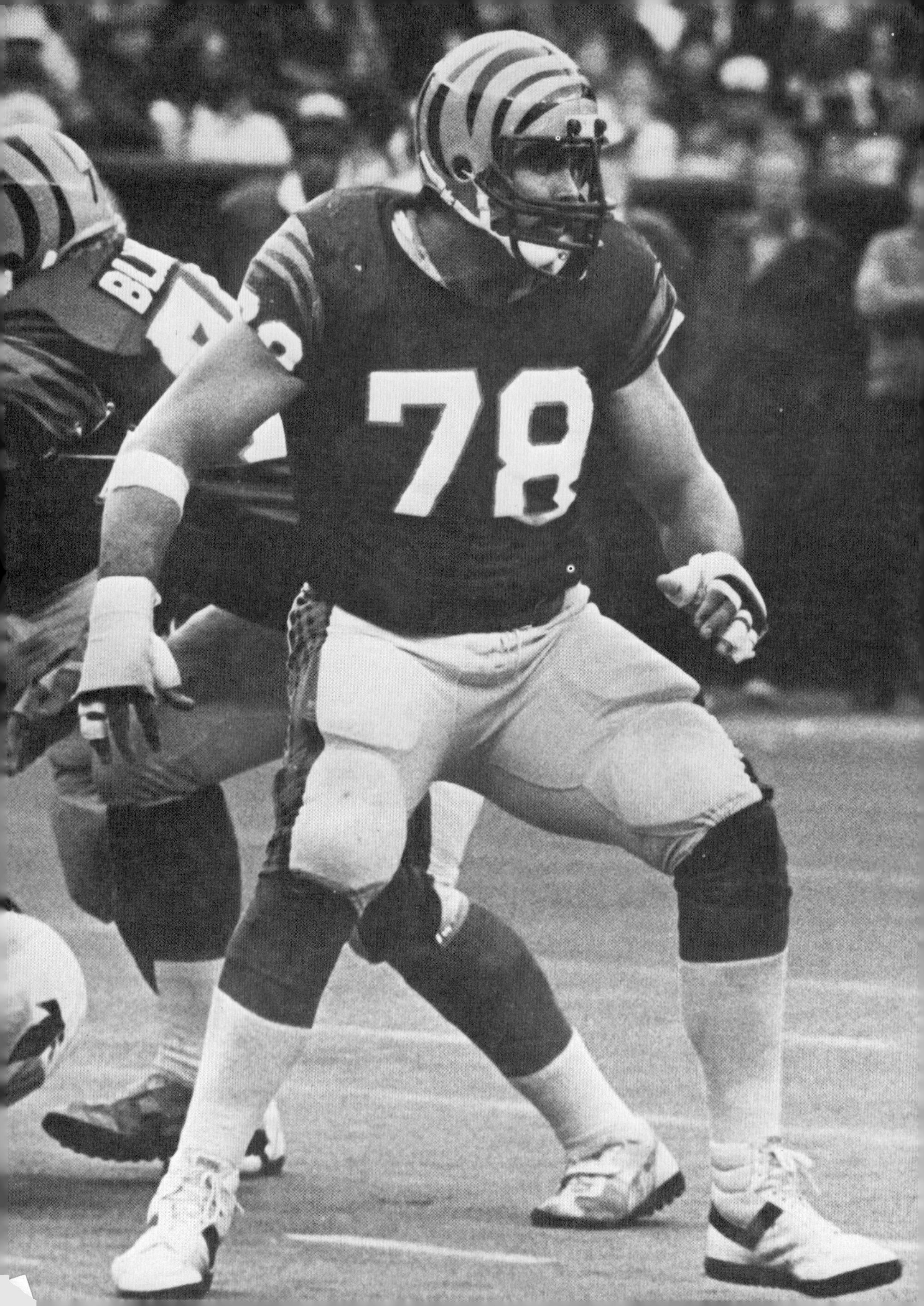
78

biggest game of all, the Super Bowl. During the final week before the big game, the store fronts throughout the city were draped in orange and black bunting. One fan even painted his car with tiger stripes!

Cincinatti's opponent would be the fancy San Francisco 49ers. Both teams knew each other well. The 49ers had been the last team to defeat the Bengals, handing them a 21-3 loss at home. This time, promised the Cincinatti fans, the story will have a different ending.

As it turned out, however, the 49ers added a few twists to the plot. Wasting no time, San Francisco QB Joe Montana marched down the field and snuck for a 1-yard TD on San Francisco's second possession. The Bengals seemed tight and jittery as if they were awed by the huge crowd inside the Pontiac Silverdome and the world-wide television audience. Like that opening game against Seattle, nothing went right for the Bengals in the first half. Montana threw for another touchdown and Ray Wersching booted two field goals for a 20-0 San Francisco lead at intermission.

Down in the Bengal dressing room, Coach Gregg pondered a difficult choice. Should he bench Anderson? Should he throw away the game plan? Or should he continue his efforts to establish the run?

"We've gotten this far behind Ken," he reasoned. "We'll live or die with him here."

The vote of confidence was just what Anderson needed. He came out throwing in the second half, mixing his receivers and confusing the 49er defense. When Collinsworth and Curtis were double-covered deep, Anderson flipped a series of soft ones to tight end Dan Ross. Anderson finished off one drive with a 5-yard

Did you know?

Turk Schonert, the young free-wheeling Bengals quarterback, will never forget a 1981 game against Seattle. With the Bengals trailing the Seahawks, 21-0, Schonert came in to replace Ken Anderson and rallied the team to a 27-21 victory!

Heading into the 1985 campaign, powerful defensive tackle Anthony Munoz was pointing towards his fourth consecutive Pro Bowl appearance.

> **Did you know?**
>
> *In 1982, quarterback Ken Anderson recorded the all-time pass completion percentage with a torrid 70.6 percent, wiping out the old mark of 70.3 percent which had been held by the legendary Sammy Baugh since 1937!*

scoring jaunt. Then his 4-yard pass to Ross cut the lead to 20-14 early in the final period. San Francisco built the lead back to 26-14, but Ross caught his second TD pass late in the contest. Now, only six points separated the Bengals from the championship.

There was silence on the Cincinnati sidelines. The Bengals were out of timeouts, and the clock was running. If they could just get the ball one more time...but Joe Montana wasn't about to let this one slip away. He ate up the clock. The final score: San Francisco, 26; Cincinnati, 21.

Forrest Gregg congratulated the men for their spirit and determination. "You guys played one heckuva second half," he reminded them. "Everyone in Cincinnati is proud of you, and you should take pride in yourselves."

Some teams never really bounce back from such a disappointing loss, but the Bengals did. In 1982, they stormed down the stretch to win six of their last seven games and claim a playoff spot once more. At times, Anderson, Ross and Collinsworth were virtually unstoppable. In the first playoff game against New York, however, the Jets found a way to keep all three under wraps. Cincinnati's hopes of a repeat Super Bowl bid were dashed early as New York won, 44-17.

THE BENGALS BUILD AGAIN

Over the next two seasons, the Bengals launched a slow, steady rebuilding program. Some of the veterans, such as reliable Ken Riley and workhorse running back

Larry "Brew" Kinnebrew, the big, power-running fullback, was the Bengals' top rusher in 1984.

Here's Eddie Edwards, one of the Bengals' sack specialists, on the attack.

Cincinnati quarterback Ken Anderson took the helm for his 15th NFL season in 1985.

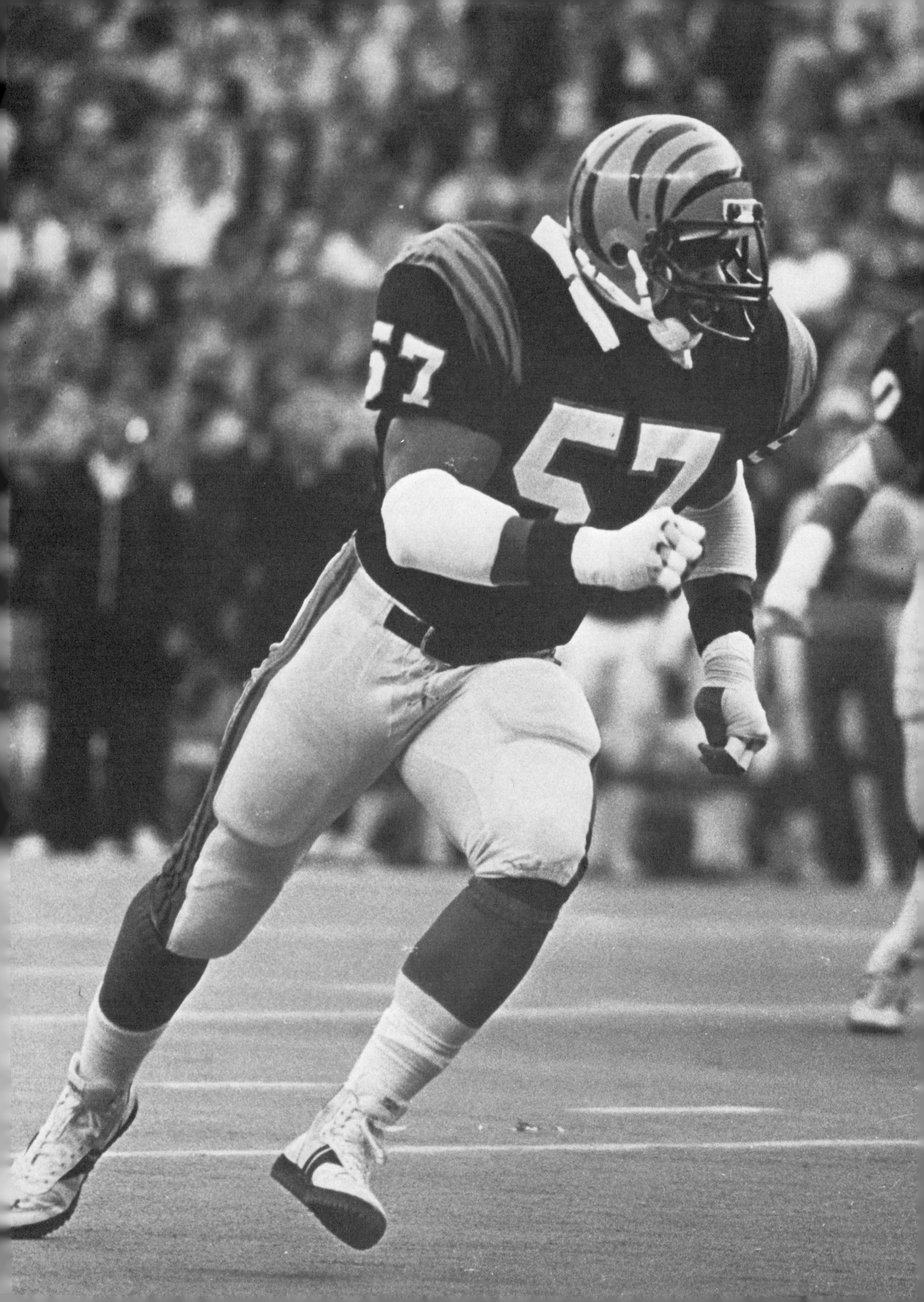

Archie Griffin, chose to retire. Other players, like Jim LeClair, Dan Ross and guard Dave Lapham, were lured to the large contracts offered by the new United States Football League.

Talented young Bengals came forward to fill the holes. Between them, tackle Anthony Munoz and center Dave Rimington brought nearly 600 pounds of power and speed to the offensive line. Ray Horton took over for Riley at cornerback. Turk Schonert and young Boomer Esiason put some positive pressure on Anderson for the quarterback spot. Heading into the 1985 season, however, Anderson remained the key man in the Bengals' offense, and for good reason.

Ken Anderson was virtually unknown when he came out of little Augustana College in 1971, but he has steadily stamped his name all over the club and league record books. Ken holds every team passing record and is now approaching the twilight zone where the very top NFL passing marks are kept. Only the legendary Fran Tarkenton and Johnny Unitas have completed more career passes than Anderson. And no QB in the game today, with the possible exception of Miami's Dan Marino, can equal the pinpoint accuracy of Anderson's passes.

After the 1981 Super Bowl loss to the 49ers, Anderson had met patiently with reporters in the Bengals dressing room. On Anderson's lap was his young son, a bright-eyed toddler dressed in Bengal orange and brown.

"We'll be back in the Super Bowl," Anderson promised the reporters as he ruffled his son's sandy hair. "Getting to the Super Bowl is nice, but winning the Super Bowl is what it's all about. I expect to be there when it happens for this team."

Did you know?

Reggie Williams, the veteran linebacker who played his entire career with the Bengals, saved some of the best for last. In 1983, Reggie made 57 unassisted tackles, 33 assists, 7.5 quarterback sacks, and recovered four fumbles!

Bengals outside linebacker Reggie Williams goes for an enemy runner in 1984 action against Seattle.

> **Did you know?**
>
> *Ricky Hunley, the Bengals' top draft choice for 1984, was drafted by the Pittsburgh Pirates baseball club in 1980. Fortunately for the NFL, Hunley decided to stick with football.*

In 1984, under new head coach Sam Wyche, Anderson and the Bengals thundered down the stretch in a valiant attempt to reach the playoffs. The sprint fell just one game short as Pittsburgh clinched the division.

With seven victories in the final nine games, however, the Bengals had gathered some critical momentum for 1985. The big cat is poised and ready to pounce. Be there to watch it happen!

Southpaw passer Boomer Esiason completed 51 of 102 passes for 530 yards and three TD's in his rookie season (1984).